Original title:
Life's Purpose? Still Working on It

Copyright © 2025 Creative Arts Management OÜ
All rights reserved.

Author: Maxwell Donovan
ISBN HARDBACK: 978-1-80566-118-4
ISBN PAPERBACK: 978-1-80566-413-0

Whispers Through the Trees

In a forest of thoughts, I roam,
Trees giggle, asking, 'Where's your home?'
Squirrels debate over acorn stocks,
While I ponder my quirky blocks.

The wind carries tales, oh so absurd,
Like a lost puppy chasing the herd.
Nature chuckles, it knows the score,
Each twist in my path, a new encore.

The Sunlit Path to Understanding

Sunlight dances on my daily grind,
While shadows of doubt lurk behind.
Chasing rainbows without a map,
I trip on socks in a friendly flap.

The daisies gossip, oh what a tease,
As I tumble down between the trees.
Finding wisdom? A slow-motion race,
With butterflies giggling, 'Pick up the pace!'

Colors of the Unexplained

Painting my dreams in vibrant hues,
Each brushstroke whispers silly clues.
Red for the coffee that spills on my shirt,
Green for the envy of my neighbor's dirt.

Orange for moments I can't quite recall,
Blue like the Monday that gave me a brawl.
Colors collide like a wild balloon,
As I dance through the chaos, a comical tune.

In Search of Lost Dreams

Hunting for dreams in an odd sock drawer,
Finding a sandwich from days of yore.
Each bite brings laughter, a taste so strange,
In a world where wishes often rearrange.

I ask my reflection for any clues,
It just smirks, suggesting I snooze.
Lost in the maze of what could have been,
With a frown turned upside down in a spin.

Flames of Inquiry

I asked a lamp about a plan,
It flickered back, 'Be a fan!'
The toaster chimed in with a toast,
'Just keep popping up, be the most!'

The fridge hummed softly, 'Stay cool, dude!'
'Chill out in life, don't be rude!'
In the chaos of appliances, I chuckled,
Ambition's just a game we all snuggled!

Halos of Hope

I wandered down a path of dreams,
Chasing after wild, silly schemes.
A squirrel yelled, 'Hey, what's your plan?'
I said, 'To be a famous pancake man!'

With each step, I tripped on fate,
A banana peel, oh, isn't that great?
Laughter echoed, despite my fall,
Turns out, fun is the best of all!

A Canvas Yet Unpainted

I bought a canvas, big and bright,
Stared at it with all my might.
Could paint a sunset, or a cat,
But ended up splattering with a splat!

The brush danced wildly, without a care,
A masterpiece? Nah, just some hair!
Yet in this mess, I found delight,
Art's not a goal, just enjoy the flight!

The Unwritten Story of Tomorrow

Tomorrow's page is blank and fresh,
Filled with chaos, and a bit of mesh.
I tried to write, but then I laughed,
    My pen decided it was daft!

The plot thickens like a foggy stew,
Characters doing what? Who knew?
In the end, it's just a funny game,
    Each day a riddle, never the same!

The Quest for Meaning

I searched for wisdom in a cookie's crack,
But only found crumbs, no guide on the stack.
With fortune's words lost in the cookie dust,
I guess my journey's just a bit of a bust.

The map I drew was scribbled and torn,
Leading through places I willingly scorn.
Perhaps I'll find answers in a good Netflix show,
Or in a dance-off with my neighbor named Joe.

Between Every Heartbeat

Counting beats while I sip my tea,
Wondering if I should just let it be.
Do I need a plan or a fancy degree?
Ah, look! A squirrel! Is it chasing me?

Mom said, 'Child, find the road that's your own,'
But I've lost my way, and I'm melted like scone.
I'll just laugh at the chaos of life I own,
Maybe tomorrow, I'll finally have grown.

Chasing Ephemeral Whispers

Whispers of fate flicker like candlelight,
They giggle and dance, then take off in flight.
I chase them with nets made of dreams and bad puns,
Yet they twirl away, like elusive little runs.

I tried to catch wisdom in a sock of unmatched,
Hoping for clarity, but I just got attached.
Next time I'll use cheese, it's a classic old scheme,
'Cause who can resist a good dairy-themed dream?

Unfinished Journeys

My map's a doodle, my compass wonky,
Taking me places that feel kind of funky.
With every turn, I laugh more than frown,
Especially when I find I'm just going 'round.

Halfway through life, I'm still at the start,
Complaining and smiling, like a work of art.
I'll skip down the path with mismatched shoes,
Who needs a big plan when you've got just the blues?

The Puzzle of Existence

In a box marked 'me,' there's a piece missing,
Perhaps it fell out while I was dismissing.
Searching for meaning in crumbs and snacks,
Guessing my fate from old pizza hacks.

The corners are weird and the lines are a blur,
I'm trying to fit in but not sure what's sure.
Assembling a picture with odd bits I've got,
Maybe it's perfect, or maybe it's not.

Instructions are vague and the colors are bright,
Every time I'm close, it slips out of sight.
But hey, there's a laugh in my puzzling plight,
Watch me juggle pieces until late at night.

So, here's to the chaos, the joy and the strife,
Piecing together this thing called a life.
A game with no rules and no clear points to score,
I'll dance with my puzzle, and maybe, just more.

Footprints in the Sand

I strolled along shores, my thoughts in a swirl,
Each step I took left a mark in a whirl.
Waves washed away my deep thoughts with glee,
"Hey, is this how existence should be?"

Seagulls squawked loudly, they seemed to agree,
Flapping their wings with wild jubilee.
I pondered my footprints, all wiggly and weird,
Turns out my path's as clear as it appeared.

The tide may erase them, that's just fine,
It's the journey that counts, not the straight line.
So, I'll skip and I'll hop, let the sand be my guide,
Laughing at life, with the ocean beside.

In every small ripple, I find pure delight,
Wandering freely into the night.
And if the tides take me, I'll just wave them goodbye,
With laughter as my compass, I'll learn how to fly.

Between the Questions and Answers

I asked if the chicken crossed first or the road,
Google just laughed and lightened my load.
"Seek not the answers, just revel in fun,
Life's quirky riddles have only begun!"

"How many socks should one have in a drawer?"
An infinite quest; I still want one more!
The laundry spins tales of misplaced myths,
Golden nuggets hiding in laundry's abyss.

Each question spins webs, full of fun and dismay,
As I tap dance around what I can't quite say.
The answers keep changing, like socks on parade,
For every new query, a new joke is made.

So I'll keep on asking, and giggling along,
What's life without quirks, a forgotten song?
With laughter as my ticket, I'll enjoy the show,
Between all the questions, let the good vibes flow.

The Map Unfurled

I spread out my map in a caffeinated haze,
With doodles and arrows to navigate my days.
"There's treasure here somewhere," I boldly declared,
As each little detour left me slightly ensnared.

My compass just spun; it clearly had dread,
Now I'm lost in the woods, but I'm well-fed.
"Which way to the laughter?" I ask with a grin,
My roadmap to joy is where the fun begins.

Mountains of worries, rivers of doubt,
But I'm sporting a smile, that's what life's about!
I'll color outside and mash up the plan,
Making my way like a whimsical man.

So here's to the map, all wrinkled and torn,
A journey of snippets and bright-colored scorn.
Each pitstop's an echo of giggles bestow,
With laughter my companion, wherever I go.

Threads of a Tattered Map

My compass spins without a clue,
An X marks where I lost my shoe.
With breadcrumbs scattered in the breeze,
I chase the squirrels, not my dreams.

I jot down notes in crayon ink,
Each doodle leads me to the brink.
A map that's drawn with squiggly lines,
Who knew that fate would run on twines?

I asked the stars for a sign or two,
They blinked at me—what should I do?
With half-filled cups and mismatched socks,
I wander freely—not on clocks.

So here I roam, a traveler bold,
In search of treasure, or so I'm told.
With laughter loud and heart so light,
I spin my wheels, it feels just right.

Echoes of Ambition

I dreamt of castles made of gold,
But tripped on shoes that looked quite old.
The echoes call, I chase the sound,
Yet here I sit, still earthbound.

Plans I penned in neon ink,
But they dissolve—oh, how they stink!
My journal filled with puns and laughs,
A blueprint full of goofy gaffs.

Ambitions grow like weeds, you see,
They sprout up fast—then flee with glee.
I plant my dreams in silly pots,
Yet veggies sprout as tangled knots.

So onward still, I grasp at air,
In search of meaning everywhere.
With chuckles loud, I skip the grind,
For joy is what I've really mined.

The Canvas of Tomorrow

With paintbrushes made of gummy bears,
I splash my thoughts without a care.
Each stroke a giggle, a wink or tease,
A canvas filled with what-ifs and wheeze.

The future wears a polka dot dress,
Sipping coffee from a glittery mess.
I canvas dreams in bursts of light,
Even when the colors don't feel right.

On this artwork of blunders and grace,
I sketch the smile on a dog's face.
With paint that runs like my wild hair,
I dance in circles, free as air.

Tomorrow's bright, or so they say,
With crayons sharp in bright array.
So I'll create and laugh anew,
For joy is what I'm meant to do.

Navigating the Questions

With maps that swirl like cotton candy,
I ask the clouds, 'Is this quite dandy?'
The compass laughs and points the way,
   To where the silly thoughts all play.

Questions bounce like bouncy balls,
Some run away through open halls.
I chase them down with fork in hand,
   To grill a truth or make a stand.

Directions given by wise old owls,
In riddles wrapped, they hoot and prowl.
I nod and smile, pretend to know,
   As I tumble down this winding road.

So here I am with snacks galore,
Still munching on what's in the store.
Navigating with giggles tight,
   Content to savor every bite.

Unwritten Chapters

I gaze at my notebook, filled with blank,
Procrastination's my secret weapon, I prank.
Each page is a canvas, yet so pristine,
Who knew my story would be so routine?

Plot twist today, I spilled coffee on dreams,
As I sip the dregs from my silly themes.
Characters dance like they've lost their way,
Heck, I may just write them a holiday!

With each new chapter, I start to fret,
How many plot holes will I manage to set?
Pencil's my partner, though it leads me astray,
At least I'm the author of this wacky play!

The ending's a mystery, or so I presume,
A twist like a snail in a cluttered room.
So here's to the chaos as I turn the page,
Life's a comedy show, and I'm on the stage.

Dreams in the Making

I've got a vision board, it's quite the sight,
Glitter and giggles from day until night.
Yet here I am, still in pajamas so old,
Chasing my dreams, politely bold.

Plans never happen on the predicted day,
Like socks in the dryer, they run far away.
I'll catch them one morning, like butterflies,
Perhaps I'll get somewhere before they go fly!

Each night I lay dreaming of striking it rich,
But morning brings laundry, what a switch!
I write my own rules, break 'em with glee,
Who says my ambitions can't take a tea?

Yet as the sun rises, I know it's a game,
Making it big is a bit of a claim.
So here's to the dreams that wiggle and squirm,
My wild heart's in charge of this hilarious term!

The Silence Between Notes

I play a tune that's just off the beat,
It sounds like a cat with gigantic feet.
The notes fly around like bees in a jar,
Each one trying hard to be a star!

I hum in the shower, I dance in my chair,
Neighbors may question, is it really fair?
But I shake my booty like there's no delay,
If music's my passion, then loud's the way!

Yet every crescendo comes with a twist,
Like trying to boil water, I can't resist.
I'll keep on playing, though chaos ensues,
As long as I'm smiling, who cares about blues?

So here's to the silence that makes us all laugh,
The rhythm of life's on my funky giraffe.
Sway with the sounds, let the magic ignite,
In this crazy concert, we'll all be alright!

Conversations with the Unknown

I talk to my shadow, it's rather profound,
It whispers back secrets without making a sound.
There's wisdom in stillness, they say it's so clear,
But usually, my shadow is just kinda weird!

The moon chuckles softly as I ask for advice,
It's brilliant, yet cold, and not very nice.
"What's my next step?" I ponder at night,
Its glimmering laughter is always polite.

I try to converse with the clouds overhead,
But they drift and they float, leaving me with dread.
"Hey, help with my plans, don't just disappear!"
It tickles my thoughts, now I'm stuck here.

Yet still I persist in seeking the wise,
From random musings to poetic highs.
In this playful chatter, I find my own space,
A blend of confusion, a whimsical chase.

The Tapestry of Dreams

Stitching hopes with threads of cheer,
Every goal seems crystal clear,
Yet I trip on all my schemes,
Falling into Monday's memes.

With colors bright and patterns odd,
I craft my fate, a little flawed,
A quilt of wishes, here and there,
Turns out I've made a comfy chair!

Dreams unravel, oh what a sight,
I can't tell if it's day or night,
Maybe I'll nap, just for a while,
And wake up with a brand new style!

So raise a glass to twists and turns,
Where laughter's gold and hope still burns,
In this fabric, life's a joke,
I'm the punchline; can't you poke?

Still Climbing the Mountain

I'm scaling heights, forgetting snacks,
With every step, there's more to pack,
A summit view, or so they say,
But first, I've lost my way today!

Each rock I trip on tells a tale,
Of times I thought I'd surely fail,
But laughing helps, so up I go,
On craggy paths, I steal the show!

Why do they talk of peaks so grand?
I'd rather picnic on the sand,
Yet here I am, still grinning wide,
Fumbling up this mountain-side!

So pack your bags and join my spree,
We'll find some sunshine, you and me,
For in the climb, we stretch and grow,
And maybe fall; but hey, that's how!

Mornings of Reflection

The morning sun spills out my dreams,
Over coffee, life's not as it seems,
I ponder why my toast won't pop,
Is that the sign I should just stop?

The clock ticks loud, a silly beat,
As thoughts parade, oh what a feat,
I chase my thoughts, like ducks in line,
But they just quack, and sip my wine!

Should I be grand, or just pretend?
Each sip of brew feels like a trend,
But really, who can understand,
The mystery of spilled milk and sand?

So here I sit, reflecting wide,
With mismatched socks and dreams tied tight,
If answers come, I'd love to see,
But first, let's laugh at our coffee spree!

Pieces of a Soul's Mosaic

I'm piecing bits, like jigsaw art,
Confused and lost, where do I start?
Each shard shines bright, with flaws in tow,
A masterpiece? Or just a show?

With glue that drips and colors clash,
I scramble fast, oh what a bash,
This patchwork heart has stories grand,
Of times I tripped—not what I planned!

Yet every piece tells tales of laughs,
Quirky moments, like silly gaffs,
Embrace the mess, I wholeheartedly claim,
It's way more fun than playing the blame!

So here's to all the pieces lost,
To finding joy, at any cost,
In this odd craft, I'm not alone,
We'll share the fun; let's make it known!

Shadows of Intention

In a world where I roam free,
Trying to find the best me.
Chasing dreams like a wild hare,
But I often find I'm not quite there.

Chasing goals that come and go,
Like socks that vanish in the flow.
Coffee in hand, I strike a pose,
Yet my laundry pile only grows.

I ponder and muse with great flare,
While snacks sneak in without a care.
Plans collide like a bumper car,
But laughter echoes near and far.

So here's to the quest, the silly chase,
With googly eyes and a painted face.
Maybe I'll find what's meant to be,
Or just enjoy the fun of me!

Falling Leaves and New Beginnings

The leaves drop down in twirls and spins,
In this game, sometimes I lose and win.
With each season, a dance anew,
Yet still not sure just what to do.

In the fall, I get to cozy,
But my ambitions feel a bit nosy.
Pumpkin spice and all that jazz,
Yet I'm stuck in a tangled whazz.

Winter's chill brings a blanket of clout,
As I ponder what this fuss is about.
Hot cocoa in hand, wrapped snug and tight,
Wondering if I'm doing it right.

Spring will come, with blooms to flaunt,
And I'll try again, this I do want.
With laughter and cheer, I'll take my shot,
Finding new dreams within each pot!

The Tides of Inner Landscapes

Waves crash in my mind like a show,
Where thoughts ebb and flow, never slow.
I try to ride the current with glee,
But sometimes I just want a cup of tea.

The sandcastle plans, they collapse and break,
Building towers feels like quite the mistake.
Yet I laugh at the mess, what's done is done,
Embracing the chaos, having some fun.

Seagulls squawk with opinions so loud,
As I wade through this quirky crowd.
I shout back, "I'll figure it out!"
While they circle my head with a peck and a pout.

So let's grab a surfboard, ride that wave,
In this vast ocean, we're all just brave.
With a splash, I'll dive into the unknown,
For in this tide, I've surely grown!

Reflections in Still Waters

A mirror calm, the water's just right,
I gaze at my face, oh what a sight!
With thoughts that ripple and twist away,
What am I doing, come what may?

Ducks quack their wisdom with teasing delight,
As I ponder my dreams by day and night.
"Just float along," they seem to say,
While I'm splashing on this crazy play.

Reflections twirl, like a dancer so spry,
Yet I sometimes flail and wonder why.
"Is this my path?" I laugh in the dew,
Maybe it's just too much to chew.

So here's to the water, calm and bright,
And to the giggles that fill my flight.
As I toss a pebble, let it fall wide,
I'll splash in the ripples, it's quite the ride!

Veils of Tomorrow

In the morning I wake up late,
Dreaming of eggs, not my fate.
I trip on my socks, what a sight,
Coffee's my guide, oh what a plight.

Chasing my dreams like a cat and a mouse,
While fending off chores in my cluttered house.
I ponder my goals, they seem to elude,
Is adulting just one giant riddle or feud?

With plans in my pocket, and snacks in my hand,
I'm off on a quest that's just barely planned.
I'll conquer the world, or take a short nap,
Who needs a map? A good sandwich will snap!

Peeking at life through a foggy lens,
Juggling my whims, making new friends.
Perhaps I'll find meaning in pizza and fries,
Or in laughter found in the silliest ties.

Emblems of Curiosity

With questions like fireflies, I roam,
Buzzing through life, far from home.
Why does the toaster only burn bread?
Or do I sleepwalk? I'm laden with dread.

I search for the answers beneath my bed,
Where lost thoughts and socks all mingle instead.
My quest for knowledge, a delightful fun spree,
Why is the sky blue? Just let it be!

Eating my cereal, I ponder and muse,
Silly thoughts dancing like colorful shoes.
Do ducks know they quack, or is it just fate?
Questions abound as I contemplate weight.

So I scribble these thoughts in a notebook so dear,
Like a squirrel with acorns, I gather my cheer.
One day I'll know, with a laugh or a sigh,
Until then, I'll keep asking—Oh my, oh my!

The Construct of Being

Building a life like a house made of cards,
Every little wind just sends me off yards.
Blueprints I drew turned to doodles in haze,
Yet still I construct, through this curious maze.

My neighbors, they laugh, can they see my grand plan?
Or are they just puzzled by this curious man?
Each brick is a question, a humorous tale,
Of locating the keys to this mystical scale.

I slap on some paint, like a clown in a booth,
Creating a façade, searching for truth.
Am I architect, builder, or just a stray cat?
In a world full of blueprints, I'm all over that!

With laughter as mortar, I hold it all tight,
Fumbling through life in this comical flight.
So here's to the jigsaw, the pieces that sway,
I'll build what I can, come what may!

A Journey of Fibonacci

In a world of numbers, I'm lost in a sum,
Fibonacci whispers, 'Please don't be dumb!'
One plus one equals a little sweet bee,
The way that I buzz puts a smile on me.

Counting my days like the petals of blooms,
Each petal's a giggle, erasing the glooms.
Trying to follow this spiral of fun,
While tripping on tangents, I'm still on the run.

The rabbit's so clever, hop-hopping along,
With patterns and rhythms, life's still a song.
But if two's a crowd, what's the rule of three?
My math may be fuzzy, yet so wild and free!

So I dance with the odds, embracing the jest,
In this number game, I'm doing my best.
Who needs to know what the formula be?
Just counting my laughs, that's enough for me!

Unspoken Dialogues

In the mirror I converse, my hair's a mess,
The toothpaste spills as I must confess.
Hobbies? Dream jobs? A real pickle here,
Navigating choices with a side of beer.

The cat gives me looks, like I'm not quite right,
While I ponder my options late into the night.
Should I bake a cake or learn to paint skies?
Can't promise I'll choose; I might just improvise.

The Labyrinth of Wishes

I chased a big dream; it ran away fast,
Like a cat with a laser beam—what a blast!
With forks in the road, I take a wrong turn,
For every wrong wish, there's a lesson to learn.

I penned down my goals, then tossed them aside,
I think I'll just nap; let the universe decide.
In this wacky maze of hopes that I weave,
I smile at the twists and the traps that deceive.

Embracing Uncertainty

Got a plan, then it vanished, like socks in the wash,
I embrace the unknown with a goofy little posh.
Why play it straight when I can take a detour?
With my compass spinning, I guess there's allure.

Uncertainty's dance is quite hard to master,
Like trying to race while you're stuck in a plaster.
So I'll twirl with the whims and giggle at fate,
Making up fun moves, oh isn't this great?

Whispered Aspirations

I whispered my dreams to the fridge late at night,
It hummed back advice—oh, what a delight!
By morning I'd changed my ideas again,
What's the difference between a llama and zen?

I plan with excitement, but then start to yawn,
Who knew that ambitions could be so withdrawn?
With a sigh and a chuckle, I throw in the towel,
Tomorrow I'll try—after binge-watching a howler.

Searching for North Star

Woke up today, felt a bit lost,
Thought I'd find wisdom at any cost.
Head turned sideways, like a confused pup,
Google Maps can't help, I'll erupt!

A compass spins like a party balloon,
While I ponder life under a bright full moon.
With snacks in hand, I wander around,
In search of a star that won't be found.

My friends suggest following my heart,
But my heart just says, 'Let's go eat tarts!'
So here I am, on this silly quest,
Laughing at signs that say, 'Just God bless!'

Perhaps I'll just take a nap in the park,
Dream of wisdom till it gets dark.
Life's a puzzle, and I'm in a fog,
But at least I've got snacks and my dog!

Echoes of a Silent Heart

Saw a deep thought, it whispered my name,
But when I spoke back, it played a game.
With every answer, I scratched my chin,
Is this a riddle, or just noise within?

Journals lay scattered, pages askew,
Filled with questions that sound like a zoo.
Dear heart, stop echoing, lend me a hand,
Or I'll launch into outer space, unplanned!

Each tick of the clock, I'm brewing a brew,
Add sugar, spice, and an existential screw.
I laugh with the echoes, oddly profound,
But I'd rather be laughing with friends all around.

So here's to the echoes that make us think,
While I chew on thoughts with my drink.
In this silence, I'm finding my way,
Even if I trip on a wordplay!

Through the Labyrinth of Time

Lost in time, where did it go?
Tick-tock, tick-tock, is that my show?
Running through circuits, I trip and I slide,
Like a mouse in a maze, I'm high on pride.

I ask the wise owl for directions clear,
But it hoots 'bout trifles I can't adhere.
With each wrong turn, I chuckle and laugh,
What's the point if I don't find the path?

As clocks spin wild, I throw up my hands,
Maybe I'll dance with the time-woven bands.
Clockwise or counter, who says it's a race?
A waltz in the labyrinth is my best place.

So here's to the questions that float in the air,
Like balloons that drift without a care.
With whimsy and giggles, I march down the line,
Laughing with time, it's all by design!

Striving for the Unseen

I reached for the moon, but got a bug bite,
It seems the stars are quite out of sight.
With a telescope, I glance at the dark,
What's out there? Just a shooing spark.

I ask my goldfish, what's the big deal?
He just swims in circles, no thoughts to reveal.
Making plans to catch clouds in a net,
Turns out, I'm just a lovely mess, I bet!

Chasing dreams like they're socks in the wash,
Each time I wash, they flee with a swash.
Yet here I am, with smiles on my face,
Finding humor in this race without pace.

Maybe one day I'll see the unseen,
But till then, I'll sip through the routine.
With joy in my heart, I'll keep pushing ahead,
Even if it means chasing crumbs of bread!

Footprints in the Sand

I walked along the shore one day,
My footprints washed away, oh what a play!
Thought I'd leave a mark, bold and grand,
But the tide just chuckled, "Not on my land!"

Seagulls squawk with a teasing grin,
"Where's your plan? Oh, let's begin!"
I waved them off, they took to flight,
"Who needs a map? I'll be alright!"

With every step, I second guess,
Is this the path? Or just a guess?
The sand shifts softly beneath my toes,
A dance of fate, who really knows?

So with happy heart, I stroll right on,
A wandering soul, from dusk till dawn.
No need for signs, I'll make it fun,
Just me, the beach, and the gleaming sun!

The Art of Becoming

Each day I wake, what's on the slate?
A selfie? A snack? I just can't wait!
My coffee's brewing, a masterpiece in hand,
A caffeine buzz that's perfectly planned.

"Brush your teeth!" says my inner guide,
But I'm busy dreaming of a joyride.
Finding my vibe, seeking the thrill,
Turns out the journey's the best part still!

Dressing up like a funhouse clown,
Strutting my style, I'll wear my crown.
Is this grown-up? Well, it's unclear,
But at least I'm laughing when I steer!

So here's to missteps and little quirks,
To becoming something amidst all the works.
Life's an art and I'm the brush,
Painting it bright with giggles and hush!

Fragments of a Wondering Mind

Thoughts flutter by like paper planes,
Each one carrying laughter, joy, and pains.
"What's next?" I ponder, eyes to the sky,
Then trip on my shoelaces; oh my, oh my!

Ideas tumble like socks in a dryer,
Whirling around with a spark of desire.
One's about coffee, another a cat,
And I'm on a quest to find my own hat!

Questions bubble like soda on ice,
"Am I too silly? Or just too nice?"
My mind's a circus, wild and bright,
With clowns juggling hopes in the pale moonlight.

So here I am, a curious fool,
Seeking the magic, breaking the rule.
My fragments dance, they wiggle and squirm,
In this big adventure, I'll learn to affirm!

Skies of Possibility

What's up there? A question I pose,
Are those clouds filled with dreams, or just woes?
An airplane zips by, I wave it on,
Chasing my thoughts from dusk until dawn.

Up, up, and away like a balloon in flight,
Floating on whims in the soft moonlight.
Is today a breakthrough, or just a routine?
Who really knows what tomorrow will glean?

My brain's like a kite, tugging on string,
Dancing with hopes, oh, what will it bring?
In the sky of maybes, I twirl and spin,
With every thought, I let the fun begin.

So here's to exploring this vast open air,
With laughter and wonder, I'll not despair.
Under the skies of limitless might,
I'll find my way with a giggle and light!

Navigating the Wanderlust

My suitcase sings of hope and dreams,
But I forget my pants, or so it seems.
With maps in hand, I roam the streets,
Yet often trip on my own two feet.

My compass spins in dizzy circles,
I cross my fingers, avoid the hurdles.
Every detour holds a lesson worth gold,
But hey, my socks are mismatched and bold!

Wanderlust's call is a siren's song,
But I can't tell right from wrong.
Each step I take is a leap of faith,
Could life be a joke? A cosmic wraith!

I'll dance with my coffee cup in hand,
Each sip a clue to the master plan.
Yet sometimes I wonder, over tea,
Is finding the point just too tricky for me?

The Quest for Meaning

I put on my hat, I grab my map,
Hoping to find the meaning in a nap.
With coffee brewed strong, I take a sip,
And ponder hard while my mind does flip.

I search for signs 'neath a cosmic sky,
But all I find are clouds and pie.
Is the meaning hidden in chocolate cake?
Or is it wrapped in a silly handshake?

Each book I read just leads to more,
Questions pile high like laundry on the floor.
Philosophers chat like they've got a clue,
While I sit here just puzzled too!

So here's my quest—oh what a ride!
With laughter and snacks by my side.
I'll roam this world like a jester in flight,
Finding giggles, perhaps that's the light!

In Search of Tomorrow's Light

Each dawn brings hope, but snooze it goes,
I dream of tacos or garden gnomes.
The sunlight whispers beneath my bed,
'Get up, you silly! Time's ahead!'

With coffee splash and socks askew,
I wander forth in fuzzy shoes.
Searching for wisdom, or just breakfast,
Either way, I'm on this quest!

Will today bring answers to my plight?
Or just more snacks and a nap tonight?
The future's bright, or that's what they say,
But I think I'll just wing it today!

So here's to joy in each tangled mess,
With laughter as my finest dress.
Tomorrow's light is just a laugh away,
Let's dance and giggle till the end of day!

The Journey Within

I ventured inside, what's this I find?
A tangle of thoughts that's truly blind.
My mind's a circus of ideas so bold,
But the popcorn's burnt and the clowns are old.

Peering deeper with a curious eye,
Searching for answers, I just sigh.
Do I unpack my feelings or just take a nap?
Ah, who can tell in this funny trap?

There's wisdom hidden in each silly sock,
And epiphanies waiting to knock.
But my heart just giggles, 'let's just create,
A buffet of mischief on this plate!'

So here's the journey, with punchlines galore,
Each awkward moment, I surely adore.
With humor and grace, I'll make it through,
Finding treasure in laughter, just like you!

Beneath the Surface

I pondered long on where I fit,
But all I found was an empty bit.
Where's my map, I surely need,
To locate the path from thought to deed.

I asked a fish about the sea,
It winked and swam away from me.
'What do you know?' I called out loud,
It bubbled back, 'Too lost in the crowd.'

I dreamt of climbing a mountain high,
But why so steep? Oh, my oh my!
With every step, I trip and fall,
Maybe the ground is my best mate, after all.

In search of meaning, I made a cake,
But only ended up with a sad mistake.
With icing woes and a flour cloud,
At least my dog thinks I'm pretty proud!

The Mirror of Experience

I gazed into wisdom's bright glass,
Reflecting my thoughts like silly grass.
'What's my purpose?' I did reflect,
It laughed and said, 'That's not what I project.'

I bought a book on expert advice,
Turned out to be about cooking rice.
Clanking pots made it hard to write,
So I enjoyed a dinner done just right.

Then I tried asking an old wise man,
He shrugged and said, 'Just do what you can.'
With one shoe on and one shoe off,
Was he joking, or was that a scoff?

In laughter's hall, I danced and twirled,
Stripped of ideals, my dreams unfurled.
In every giggle and gentle spin,
I learned that the chase is where joy begins!

The Seekers' Odyssey

One day I set off with a curious mind,
Searching for answers, of every kind.
Maps in hand and snacks in tow,
But guess where my adventure chose to go?

Found a wise owl under a tree,
Asked for truth, and it hooted, 'Meh!'
With a wink, it flew off in a flurry,
While I stood there, wrapped up in worry.

I tried yoga, hoping to find zen,
Twisted and turned, but fell down again.
Meditation promised me peace galore,
I snored my way through, but learned to snore more.

So here I am, a seeker still,
Chasing the thrill with a mighty will.
In every stumble and giggling fall,
Perhaps that's the secret, after all!

Scribbled Notes on Humanity

I jotted down thoughts on a napkin bright,
About what it means to find your light.
But at lunchtime, it slipped out of sight,
And now I'm left with leftovers, last bite.

I asked a chicken, 'Why did you cross?'
It scratched its head, 'You're the real boss.'
Adventures have pecked me, oh so much,
Yet somehow, I still yearn for a touch.

Tried writing songs to find my tune,
But the only thing I caught was a spoon.
It clanged and clattered in perfect rhyme,
And now I'm offbeat, but that's just fine!

So, here's to the notes, the laughter we share,
Searching for meaning, floating through air.
In every blunder and all that strife,
We scribble our tales—what a funny life!

A Mosaic of Moments

I woke up late again today,
My coffee's strong, my hair's at play.
I dance with socks upon the floor,
Was that a dream or something more?

My cat demands the warmest spot,
I pondered life, forgot a lot.
A cookie crumbs my only guide,
How does one find the joy inside?

I scribble notes on napkins torn,
Am I a queen, or just a scorned?
A puzzle made of mismatched themes,
In search of purpose, or just dreams?

Yet, laughter's found in every chance,
In silly moves, we find our dance.
So here I stand, quite out of place,
A mosaic made of time and space.

Threads of Infinity

I'm tangled up in life's long thread,
Is this the path to joy, I said?
My plans are scribbles on a pad,
A cosmic joke? It's just so bad!

With every twist, I knit and purl,
I seek the answers, give a whirl.
But wrinkles laugh at solid seams,
Life's tapestry is full of memes!

A sock factory of odd designs,
My laundry basket crossed the lines.
For every thread I thought I knew,
I find life's fabric has quite a view!

Yet as I tug on each loose end,
I find a laugh - it's hard to mend.
So grab a stitch and hold on tight,
These threads of infinity take flight!

Amongst the Stars

I ponder planets late at night,
Are they just dots or cosmic sights?
A shooting star, I blew a wish,
To find the answer in a fish!

The cosmos sparkled with surprise,
But hiccups filled my hungry eyes.
Do aliens laugh at our proud show?
Or do they ponder, 'Where's the dough?'

While riding comets through the dark,
I left my notes upon a lark.
What's life about? I scratch my head,
And trip on thoughts that must be fed!

Yet here I am, a quirky star,
With thoughts that travel near and far.
So laugh with me beneath this sky,
Together, we'll just wonder why!

The Art of Unknowing

In my messy room of wild attempts,
I question 'why' amidst the crumbs.
With every doodle on the way,
I create my art in shades of gray.

Each failed plan's a masterpiece,
My mind's a jigsaw, pieced with fleece.
The fridge hums secrets, like a bard,
As I contemplate my garden yard.

The popcorn pops, ideas collide,
Can silly thoughts help guide my ride?
A cactus grows without a clue,
Just like me, yet strong and true!

So here's to chaos, fun, and cheer,
Where art of laughing turns the fear.
In all the chaos, I still roam,
In the paradox, I find my home.

Beyond Closed Doors

Behind the door, there's a shoe,
Mixed with dust and a broken cue.
I ponder here, what could it be?
A treasure trove? Or just more laundry?

Found some snacks from the end of the year,
And a sock that's fostering a lot of fear.
I wonder if choices hide under the mat,
Like my keys, my wallet, and that old cat.

The Seeds We Sow

Planted dreams in the backyard,
Watered them with hopes, not very hard.
But what grew sprung up with a twist,
A garden of puns that I can't resist!

Had seeds for wisdom, but what went wrong?
Got weeds of doubt, singing their song.
Can't tell if it's growth or a mess of grass,
Maybe next year, I'll just stick to sass.

A Map to Somewhere

I found a map marked with an X,
Promised adventure, maybe some flex.
But turns out it leads to a local shop,
For pizza and tacos, I had to stop!

My compass spins to the fridge this time,
Navigating snacks is my new prime.
No great expedition is in sight,
Just a map to the couch and snacks tonight.

Cracks in the Shell

Life is an egg, kinda cracked and fried,
It wobbles and shakes, can't be my guide.
Thought I had wisdom, a yolk of gold,
Turns out it's just the same old mold!

I'm cracking jokes while I'm cracking shells,
Trying to find meaning that jives and dwells.
With each little chip, I'm just being me,
A breakfast joke wrapped in mystery.

The Infinite Quest

I wake each day with grand intent,
But all I do is search for rent.
My coffee's strong, my plans are grand,
Yet here I sit, with donut in hand.

I chase my goals, they run away,
Like socks that vanish in the fray.
I scribble notes, a to-do list,
But finding purpose? Oh, I missed!

The cat looks wise, he judges me,
With every purr, he makes me see.
His simple life, so full of bliss,
While I search through the endless abyss.

Perhaps the answers lie in cake,
Or maybe next week's big mistake.
For now, I'll laugh and take a break,
And eat my weight in chocolate flake.

A Script Yet to be Penned.

I planned a life that's full of thrills,
But all I got are endless bills.
With every plot twist, laughter's near,
As I fumble through, fueled by fear.

I thought I'd write my epic tale,
Instead, I'm stuck in an email trail.
My characters are just my friends,
Who giggle at my awkward bends.

Cue the drama, cue the strife,
A comedy of daily life.
In every mess, a lesson learned,
But still I fumble, badly burned.

So here's the script, it's still undone,
With bloopers galore—it's all in fun.
I'll grab some popcorn, take a seat,
And watch my chaos on repeat.

Searching for North Stars

I gaze at the sky, searching for signs,
But all I find are blinking lines.
The GPS says, 'You have arrived,'
Yet here I am, still unthrived.

I tried to map out my grand design,
But all I traced were spaghetti lines.
With every step, I trip and fall,
Where did I put my sense of call?

The compass spins, it has a laugh,
While I'm just searching for a path.
I ask the moon with hopeful glee,
But all it whispers is 'Just be free!'

So here I wander, through night and day,
With mismatched socks and thoughts of play.
I'll dance along this winding way,
And hope one day I'll find my sway.

In the Garden of Dreams

I planted seeds of grand ambition,
But all I grew was indecision.
With weeds of doubt, they start to sprout,
I water hopes, then twist and shout.

The daisies laugh at what I strive,
While I can't remember how to thrive.
In this garden, chaos reigns supreme,
Weeds are winning; it's no longer a dream.

Yet sunshine peeks through cloudy skies,
With butterflies that dance and rise.
A gentle nudge, a tickle, a grin,
I chuckle softly, letting joy in.

So here I dig through dirt and schemes,
Planting laughter among my dreams.
In every bloom, a lesson found,
That joy can sprout upon this ground.

Lighthouses in the Fog

In a world that's hazy, I roam,
Finding lighthouses I call home.
They flicker and dance, yet seem unsure,
Like me with a plan, can't quite endure.

I wave at the boats, they wave back too,
Sailing through life with no compass, boo!
Foghorns blow loudly, but what do they mean?
Maybe it's just a rude seagull, obscene!

I climb to the tower, it's a long climb,
Contemplating reasons and rhythms of rhyme.
The waves whisper secrets, so salty and sly,
I'm here for the laughs, not to ask why.

So let's raise a toast to the fog and the sea,
For guiding lost ships, perhaps you and me.
When the sun breaks through, we'll cheer and we'll sing,
For laughter is what we're discovering.

Foraging for Clarity

With a basket in hand and a map on my knee,
Searching for clarity, where could it be?
Amidst all the weeds, and the berries so bright,
Oh look, a distraction! Just my silly plight.

Mushrooms and truffles, they beckon me close,
But what if I gather a mushroom that's gross?
I'll forage for wisdom beneath leafy trees,
While dodging the squirrels, who just want my cheese!

I interview daisies, asking them stuff,
"Do you know where clarity hangs out? Is it rough?"
But they just giggle, their petals all twirl,
Guess I'll just take a nap in this nature swirl!

So, back to the basket, I toss in my pride,
No answers in sight, but I'm still on this ride.
Laughter and snacks, now that's quite a score,
Maybe clarity's just at the snack bar door!

The Heart's Silent Business

My heart runs a shop, but the doors are so tight,
It's filled with ideas that hide out of sight.
"Open up!" I shout, but it only just sighs,
With a wink and a grin, it plays secretive lies.

It sells dreams in jars, and some whimsical hopes,
But sometimes, it stocks only slippery slopes.
"How do I sell this?" I ponder in vain,
The heart just chuckles, it loves this sweet game!

Unruly transactions of laughter and tears,
Checkout lines tangled with whimsical fears.
Is it normal to barter with my wishful thoughts?
My heart keeps its secrets, it's all it's got!

So here's to the heart, with its silent decree,
While the shop's full of chaos, it keeps life breezy.
I'll dance with my heartbeat, whatever it sells,
For laughter's the currency in all of our spells!

Weaving Threads of Intention

With a loom made of wishes and ribbons of light,
I weave through the fabric, each thread feels so right.
Patterns emerge, some wobbly and fun,
Like missing a stitch in a race that I run.

Each intention I toss gets tangled with glee,
A whimsical tapestry, just let it be free!
Some days it's a rainbow, some days it's a mess,
But I giggle and smile, I refuse to stress!

Then comes a cat, pouncing right on my work,
With a flick of its tail, it gives quite a jerk.
Do I scold for destruction or laugh at the scene?
It's just a new thread, so why be so mean?

So I'll keep on weaving, let the colors collide,
With laughter and mischief, I'll let joy be my guide.
For every loose string is a chance to create,
A masterpiece woven, unplanned, but in fate!

Searching for Rays of Light

I woke up today, got out of my bed,
Pondered my mission, scratched at my head.
With coffee in hand and socks mismatched,
I took on the world, feeling quite detached.

Birds outside chirp, 'What's your grand scheme?'
I chuckle and sip, 'Oh, just chasing a dream.'
But the sun is too bright, and my plans feel so tight,
I'll just roll with the waves, hoping it feels right.

Unraveled Threads of Thought

My brain's like a sweater, a tangled old mess,
Each thought is a thread, I'm feeling the stress.
With loopy ideas and styles quite amiss,
But hey, isn't laughter a funny abyss?

I tried to untangle some grand philosophy,
But all that emerged was a bad biography.
Quirky reflections, like shoes on the roof,
I'm still wondering if that's my life's big proof.

Fleeting Moments of Clarity

A flash of insight, or maybe a joke,
I pondered the universe, then just spilled my Coke.
As clarity danced, like a cat on a wall,
It slipped through my fingers, I just had to stall.

Oh! Was that a lesson wrapped in a riddle?
Or just my tired brain playing the fiddle?
I'll chase these thoughts, though they run all around,
While snacking on chips, they can't be too profound.

The Horizon Beckons

The horizon calls out, like a friend on a quest,
But I sit on my couch, just taking my rest.
With snacks piled high and the TV aglow,
Maybe I'll ponder tomorrow's grand show.

Adventure's a spark in the mundane routine,
Yet the comfy old blanket feels warm and serene.
So I'll dream of the far, while I intend to explore,
With potato chips crunched, I'll find out for sure!

The Heart's Compass

Sometimes I feel I'm lost at sea,
With a map made of candy and a cup of tea.
I wave to the whales, and they flash me a grin,
As I sail through the waves, searching deep within.

I stumble on chests filled with socks and some cheese,
Each treasure I find gives my heart so much ease.
But the compass keeps spinning, a mischievous sprite,
Will I find my way back before it gets night?

A lighthouse of laughter shines bright on the shore,
Yet my boat's just a shoebox, a bit of a bore.
With each gust of wind, I just giggle and sigh,
Because who needs a plan when you can simply fly?

So here's to the journey, the ups and the downs,
To the bumps in the road and the silly ol' clowns.
I'll chart out my course with a wink and a cheer,
Forgetting that maps ever even appeared!

Pilgrimage of the Mind

I packed a few thoughts in my backpack of dreams,
Hiking through wisdom, or so it all seems.
But I trip on a pebble and tumble away,
While the squirrels just chuckle—oh, what a display!

I climb over ideals like rocks in the stream,
And paddle in puddles of wild thoughts and cream.
My path's paved with riddles and whispered delight,
With twists that keep tuning my brain into fright.

At the peak of my journey, I pause for a snack,
Bananas and giggles spill out from my pack.
Yet as I munch dreams, a thought buzzes through:
What on earth am I doing? I've lost me and you!

The answer's elusive, like fog on my way,
But I'll skip with the daisies, go wild and sway.
For who needs a reason to dance in the rain,
When the fun's in the frolic, not the gain?

Kaleidoscope of Intentions

Spinning through colors, my mind's quite a show,
A mishmash of wishes, just watching them flow.
I tiptoe on rainbows and slide down the light,
Finding joy in absurdity, what a silly sight!

Intentions like butterflies flap in my chest,
I try to catch one but they laugh at my quest.
I juggle my dreams like a clown at a fair,
Yet they tumble and fumble like they just don't care.

If jigsaw pieces are dreams yet not theirs,
Then what am I building with all of these layers?
The answer's a mystery, a comic delight,
So I'll cradle confusion and hold it up tight.

With every turn, I splatter the day,
Creating a mural of whimsy and play.
And if it's all nonsense, so be it, I swear,
At least I've got laughter and friends everywhere!

Ebb and Flow of Time

Tick-tock the clock, it's a playful game,
While I dance with my worries and juggle my name.
I watch as the seconds skip, hop, and leap,
While I take a quick nap and drift into sleep.

The tides have a rhythm, they pull on my thoughts,
Like ducks on a pond with some very strange knots.
Each wave rolls away, and I shout, "Hey, wait!"
Has anyone found my lost sense of fate?

As sunbeams do pirouettes in the air,
I whirl through the moments, my heart full of flair.
My calendar's bursting with plans yet unseen,
But I chase after sunsets with a grin and a bean.

So let time keep ticking, I'll march to its beat,
Collecting the laughter and dancing my feet.
And when I reach twilight, I'll cheers with a grin,
For tomorrow's another wild ride to begin!

Chasing Ambitions

I chased my dreams all day and night,
But they just laughed and took to flight.
I tried to catch them in a jar,
Turns out they're better off on Mars.

With maps and plans I set my course,
Yet often end up lost, of course.
I bought a guide, but they were wrong,
Now I'm just singing a silly song.

The pot of gold is quite a tease,
It's always just beyond the trees.
I thought I'd find it with a shovel,
But dug up nothing but trouble.

One day I'll figure out this game,
Until then, it's all the same.
With laughter as my secret key,
I'll find my way, just wait and see.

Reflections on a Fleeting Path

On this road with twists and bends,
I meet new faces, make new friends.
Some say run, while others stroll,
I just lost track of my own goal.

Potholes here, and bumps up ahead,
My GPS just shouted, 'red!'
I thought I found my guiding star,
But it turned out to be a car.

I'm fueled by snacks and strong coffee,
In search of wisdom, oh so lofty.
Yet every sign seems to mislead,
I guess it's more a garden seed.

If wandering's the name of this game,
Then count me in; it's never lame.
Let's trip and tumble, laugh at fate,
Who knows? It might just be first-rate!

Unfinished Threads of Destiny

I wove my plans with threads so bright,
But tripped on yarn in my own fight.
The tapestry still looks quite wonky,
Yet I can't help but feel a bit spunky.

My needle broke, and so did my mind,
The fabric of dreams is hard to find.
Each stitch a giggle, each knot a tear,
I'm just too tangled up in my chair.

I thought I'd knit a cozy fate,
But ended up in quite a state.
With mismatched socks and frayed ends too,
Maybe this cloth is just for the zoo.

The story goes on, despite my mess,
A patchwork quilt of pure excess.
Embrace the chaos, wear it well,
In this wild ride, we all can dwell.

Whispered Dreams of Yesterday

I heard my dreams in quiet tones,
They whispered sweetly, like old phones.
I took some notes but spilled my tea,
Now my plans are a soggy spree.

They told me to follow my heart's delight,
But it led me into a fast food fight.
With burgers stacked and fries galore,
I'm not sure what I'm searching for.

Once I sought a noble quest,
But found a couch that looked the best.
I fought with pillows that took their stand,
In the epic battle of blank and bland.

So here I sit with laughter loud,
In a fortress of snacks, feeling proud.
I'll chase my dreams, just not today,
For tomorrow's plans are in disarray.

Scatterings of Intent

I woke up today with grand designs,
A loaf of bread, perhaps some wines.
Yet here I sit, lost in my quest,
Should I nap or attempt a jest?

The plans I make all seem to fade,
Like diets gone wrong or plans delayed.
I scribble notes and take some vows,
But end up laughing at my own hows.

I chased a dream down a shopping lane,
But came back home with noodles and pain.
My purpose peeks from behind a door,
But I trip on the mat and roll on the floor.

So here I giggle, a confused soul,
As I spin around on this crazy scroll.
The journey's fun, even if it's blurred,
With each misstep, a silly word.

The Winds of Change

The winds blew softly, then they grew loud,
Promises of riches made me feel proud.
I tried to sail on my tiny boat,
But the waves declared, 'Let's rock and gloat!'

I plotted a path through a field of hay,
Thinking I'd find gold at the end of the way.
Instead, I found a dancing goat,
Who begged for snacks and stole my coat.

The breeze may shift in the light of the moon,
But finding the road often feels like a tune.
I'm stuck in a loop, a cartoon delight,
Where nothing is heavy and all feels light.

So now I drift with the wind's wild tale,
Laughing at fate; I'm ready to bail.
Change is just part of the cosmic joke,
So I'll keep floating, till I'm mere smoke.

Gathering Shoals of Wisdom

I gathered wisdom from books and screens,
But found more truth in ice cream scenes.
The deeper I delve into human plight,
The more I laugh at my clueless fright.

With friends around, we ponder and muse,
Over cups of coffee, what to choose?
We chase the thoughts that flutter like bees,
Yet most times I just nap under trees.

They say with each year, we grow more wise,
But I still can't figure out how to rise.
Each lesson learned seems to fade away,
Like socks in the dryer at the end of the day.

So here's to knowledge that's sweet and tangled,
Life's funny moments keep me all mangled.
In the end, it's the joy and not the plan,
That brings us laughter, oh, yes we can!

Puzzles Without a Picture

I found a puzzle, a jumbled mess,
With no clear picture to help my distress.
I tried to fit pieces, after a snack,
But they laughed and wiggled, saying, 'Not back!'

Each corner I picked seemed out of sync,
I pondered the chaos, then spilled my drink.
Perhaps I need a manual or guide,
But who needs a plan when you can slide?

The pieces scatter like thoughts in my head,
An abstract dance on my cluttered bed.
I stick one here, and another there,
Wondering if my brain's just lost in the air.

Yet what do I care about structured forms,
When life is a whirlwind, full of storms?
So I'll laugh at my puzzle, each quirky bit,
Finding joy in the nonsense, and calling it wit.

The Path Less Taken

I walked a road, it felt so right,
Turns out it led to a pizza fight.
With splattered sauce and merry glee,
I questioned if this was meant for me.

The GPS seemed quite confused,
It led to spots I never used.
Like chasing squirrels in the park,
While pondering if I should just embark.

But every step becomes a tale,
Of rubber ducks and ice cream trails.
So here I march, my head held high,
With every stumble, I just sigh.

Perhaps I'll find a hidden door,
Or trip on life; who could ask for more?
With every misstep, I wear a grin,
Embracing chaos, let the fun begin!

Mosaics of Misunderstanding

A puzzle piece that won't quite fit,
Like wearing socks on a hand, oh what a hit!
I asked for wisdom, got a clown instead,
Now I trip on jokes, while mostly misled.

My sage told me, 'Just follow your heart!'
But I followed my stomach, that's where I start.
Now I'm juggling burgers while trying to see,
If ketchup is love or just sticky glee.

In a world of colors, I paint too bright,
With colors of chaos, morning to night.
Each brushstroke laughs at a lesson learned,
In life's crazy canvas, I've surely turned!

So while I muddle through shapes and lines,
I'll embrace the mishaps and silly signs.
For underneath all this paint and fun,
Lies the truth that we're all on the run!

The Dance of Choices

I twirled left when I should've gone right,
Now I'm booking tickets for a chicken flight.
With confetti hats made from old newspaper,
I dance through options, a DIY caper.

The choices I make are quirky and bold,
Like trading my socks for a bag of gold.
They glitter and glimmer in a pile of dreams,
Yet often unravel at the strangest seams.

I tried to cha-cha with a pineapple too,
Said it was wise, but it just tasted blue.
Amidst the laughter, a lesson does creep,
Sometimes it's best to just laugh, not leap!

So let's foxtrot and stumble through the day,
With joyous spirit, come what may.
For life's wild dance floors are where we thrive,
In the rhythm of laughter, we truly arrive!

Seasons of the Soul

In spring, I sprout with sneezes galore,
Counting flowers like they're pesky chores.
While summer shines bright, my ice cream melts,
I plan for the winter, but forget how it felt.

Oh autumn leaves, you whirl and spin,
Like me trying to decide what's next on my kin.
Sweaters and socks are a tangled affair,
I dress like a scarecrow with fluffy hair!

Each season greets with a wink and a smile,
"Just pick a fruit or dance for a while!"
Yet in the end, as the year takes flight,
I relish the chaos, it all feels just right.

So I'll gather my seasons, both frosty and warm,
In a patchwork of moments, a very fine norm.
For amidst the seasons, my spirit will grow,
In the giggles of life, oh what a show!

www.ingramcontent.com/pod-product-compliance
Lightning Source LLC
Chambersburg PA
CBHW051631160426
43209CB00004B/595